SAINT
VALENTINE

By Ann Tompert

Illustrated by Kestutis Kasparavicius

Boyds Mills Press

Published by Boyds Mills Press, Inc.
A Highlights Company
815 Church Street
Honesdale, Pennsylvania 18431
Printed in China

First edition, 2004
The text of this book is set in 14-point Goudy.
The illustrations are done in watercolor.

Visit our Web site at www.boydsmillspress.com

10 9 8 7 6 5 4 3 2 1

Library of Congress Cataloging-in-Publication Data

Tompert, Ann.
    Saint Valentine / by Ann Tompert ; illustrated by
Kestutis Kasparavicius
    p.   cm.
    ISBN 1-59078-181-3 (alk. paper)
    1. Valentine, Saint—Juvenile literature. 2. Christian
martyrs—Italy—Rome—Biography—Juvenile literature.
[1. Valentine, Saint. 2. Saints.]   I. Kasparavicius, Kestutis.
II. Title.

BR1720.V28T66 2004
270.1'092—dc22

2003026419

For Donna and David
—A. T.

For my wife, Raimonda
—K. K.

Saint Valentine's life is a mystery.

He may have been a Roman nobleman. He may have been a doctor. He may have had a shop near the Forum, the marketplace of ancient Rome. We don't know for sure.

We do know he was born in or near Rome sometime in the third century A. D. We know he was a Christian priest during the reign of the Roman emperor Claudius II. The rest is legend.

Valentine lived during a time when Christians were considered traitors. They frequently suffered death because they refused to worship the emperor and the many Roman gods. Ever fearful of discovery, Valentine and his fellow Christians met secretly in homes or shops or sometimes even in one of the caves in the hills surrounding Rome. They may have gathered at night around a simple table. In prayerful silence, they must have watched Valentine bless bread and wine, as Christ had commanded his disciples to do in memory of his Last Supper.

According to one legend, Valentine comforted imprisoned Christians by sending them hearts cut out of parchment.

Another legend has Valentine running into trouble with the Roman authorities after Claudius issued an edict, or command, forbidding Roman soldiers to marry. Claudius believed that married men made poor soldiers because they were more loyal to their wives and children than to him.

Valentine believed the ban on military marriages was unjust. He defied the emperor and conducted secret weddings for young lovers.

When word of Valentine's actions reached Claudius, he was furious. He declared Valentine an enemy of the empire, and had him seized and thrown into jail.

Valentine languished in a harsh Roman prison. After a year, he was dragged before Claudius and a group of Roman senators, members of the empire's governing body. After Valentine admitted his guilt, Claudius, out of curiosity, asked Valentine to explain his Christian beliefs. We are told that Valentine spoke with such grace that he won the emperor's admiration and goodwill. Then Valentine rashly tried to convert Claudius to Christianity.

"Give up thy gods of wood and stone," he said, according to legend. "Accept the one true God instead. Without a doubt thy empire and rule will be more fortunate and endure longer." The senators were outraged by Valentine's words. They demanded death for this man preaching false doctrines. But Claudius wanted to spare Valentine's life. Rather than sentence him to death, he turned Valentine over to a trusted lieutenant named Asterius. He ordered Asterius to do whatever he could to make Valentine renounce his Christian beliefs and worship the Roman gods.

Asterius brought Valentine into his home, hoping to win him over with kindness. He soon discovered, however, that neither the promise of wealth nor the threat of death could make Valentine worship the Roman gods.

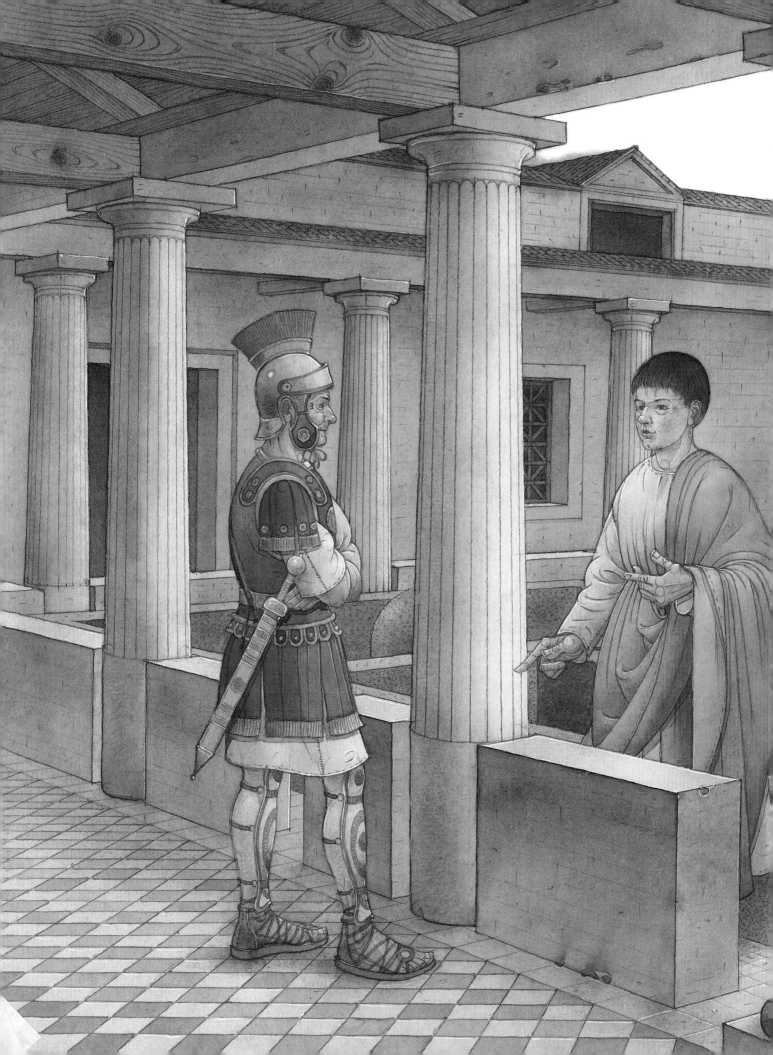

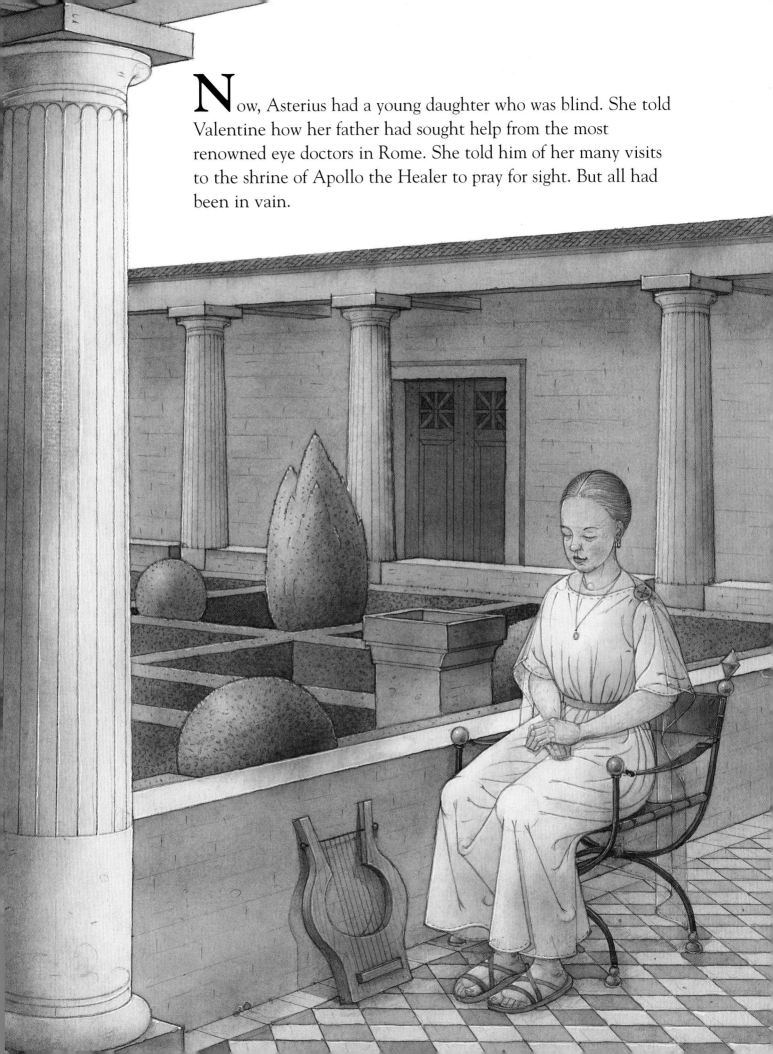

Now, Asterius had a young daughter who was blind. She told Valentine how her father had sought help from the most renowned eye doctors in Rome. She told him of her many visits to the shrine of Apollo the Healer to pray for sight. But all had been in vain.

Valentine asked Asterius if he might try to restore his daughter's sight. At first, Asterius was reluctant to doom his daughter to another disappointment. But eventually he agreed. Valentine prayed that the girl's sight be restored. According to one legend, as Valentine prayed, a bright light filled the room, and the girl was given the gift of sight.

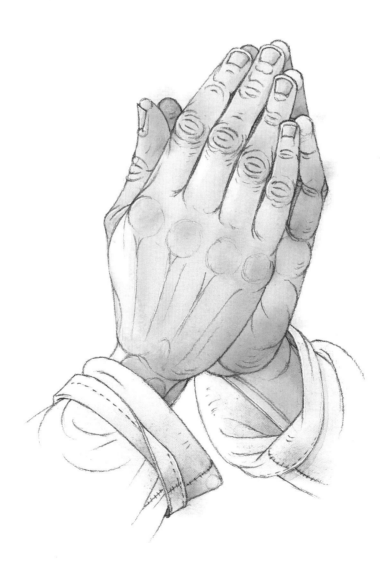

Asterius was amazed. He was convinced that Valentine's one god was more powerful than all the Roman gods put together. Valentine spent many hours speaking of the life of Christ and Christian beliefs. In time, Valentine baptized Asterius, his family, and his servants and slaves.

Upon hearing what had happened, Claudius sentenced Asterius to death along with all the Christians in his household. This time Claudius did not spare Valentine.

Tradition tells us that on February 14, around the year A.D. 270, Valentine was taken outside the Flaminian Gate on the road that runs north from Rome. There he was beheaded and buried. Afterward, the gate became known as Valentine's Gate. Later, it was renamed the People's Gate.

According to legend, an almond tree, a symbol of friendship and love, was planted near Valentine's grave. It blossomed for many years on February 14.

AUTHOR'S NOTE

Uncovering facts about Saint Valentine is difficult. During his lifetime, the Roman Empire was in a fifty-year period of military anarchy (A. D. 235–285). The average reign of an emperor was fewer than three years. Many records were either lost or destroyed.

After he was martyred, dozens of stories about Valentine circulated. While one tradition tells us that he was thrown into prison for performing secret weddings for soldiers forbidden to marry, other accounts say that he was jailed because he gave aid and comfort to persecuted Christians. He is said to have sent them hearts cut from parchment to remind them of God's love and to encourage them to remain faithful Christians. If so, this may be the origin of our use of hearts on Valentine's Day.

The story of Valentine's curing the blind daughter of Asterius and the subsequent conversion of Asterius, his wife, and all his household to Christianity was widely circulated. One legend tells us that he sent the daughter of Asterius a farewell message signed "From your Valentine." If true, it probably was the origin of an expression that has been used million of times over the centuries.

Just why we send messages of friendship and love on February 14, Saint Valentine's feast day, is not historically clear. But for hundreds of years people have set aside that day to give special attention to those they love and cherish. What better way to honor the memory of that brave Christian, Saint Valentine?

One of the earliest accounts of Saint Valentine's life was included in the *Nuremberg Chronicle*, published in Germany in 1493. Much of the same material can be found in *Butler's Lives of the Saints*, originally published around 1756. In writing this biography, I used a revised edition published in 1981. Additional information came from *Lives of the Saints* by Alfonso Villiegas, written in Spanish in 1630 and later translated into English and Italian.